Unfolding
a Lost World

by

Joy Barratt

Expressions Press
2017

Unfolding a Lost World

Produced and printed in:
Mission, British Columbia, Canada
ISBN 978-1-7750095-0-4

Expressions Press
PO Box 148
Mission
British Columbia
Canada
V2V 1A0

for my family,
as legacy

with heartfelt thanks
to
Frances Stewart
Catharine Parr Traill
and
Susanna Moodie
for writing their journeys,
folding them up,
and sending them off.

Table of Contents

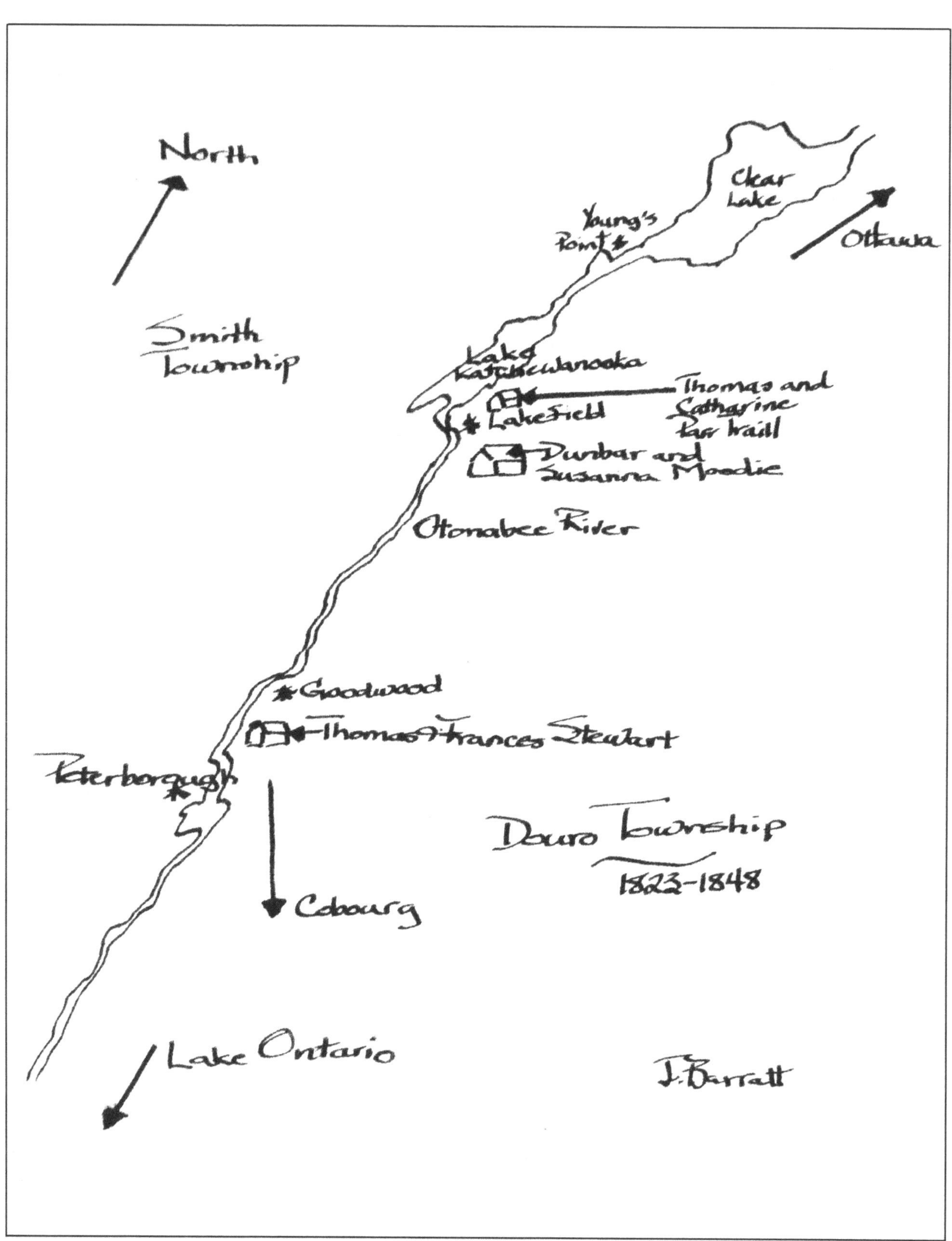

The location of the writers, Ontario, Canada, 1800s.

To The Reader

Unfolding a Lost World was conceived as a series of interfolded poetic interpretations of letters written almost two hundred years ago by a trio of original settler women.

With their husbands and children, Frances, Susanna and Catharine began the settlement of the Peterborough area of Upper Canada, now the province of Ontario. The first of the three, Frances Stewart, arrived from Ireland in 1822. She was followed by the two Scottish sisters, Catharine Parr Traill and Susanna Moodie, a decade later. These women, uniquely among the immigrants of that time, wrote elaborate, numerous and illuminating letters back to their families in Ireland and Scotland.

My original idea of re-presenting their experiences in the found-poem form was a publication that would require the reader to open their long-lost messages from envelope-like folds. This physical form, however, proved far too costly to produce in number, as each book had to be folded, bound and covered by hand. After great toil, a dozen hand-made versions do exist. The whole venture had to be re-imagined in regular book form, such as you have now here in your hands, under the same title, in order to improve accessibility of the work.

Though you readers of this perfect-bound version have been denied the sensual pleasure of opening, in the same manner as the original recipients of the letters, these fragments of long-ago life, often harrowing and all-taxing of inner resolve and emotional resilience, it is my sincere wish that what you see here will remind you of these ladies' courageous natures. For, thanks to these three, and others of their ilk who dared to dream awake a "better" life in the far wilderness reaches of North America, our Canada has prospered.

Joy Barratt

Cabin Fevered

from:
Revisiting "Our Forest Home,"
The Immigrant Letters
of Frances Stewart,
Two letters, July and August, 1822

Unfolding "Cabin Fevered"

Hundreds of thousands of immigrants must have experienced the disorienting and wrenching sensation of watching as the shores of their native land receded from view. For early settler women, that sensation would have been even more poignant as they realized the finality of their loss: all that had been familiar, family, friends, and even of other women as companions. Aboard ship, they were additionally isolated and minimized by the immense skies and the unending ocean. Confined by deck, rails, cabin walls and berths where their flesh was virtually pressed to a stranger's, by bunked restraint in stormy weather and mind-bending stagnation in becalmed seas and by the unknown rocks which tore at the vessel's hull, they were sustained only by a vision of a better life. I have tried to picture all these sentiments in this poem in which the only un-caged creatures are the sharks, petrels, shearwaters and porpoises.

pettrils pettrils pettrils

Shearwaters Shearwaters Shearwaters

Brig Geo. Thompson: 2nd - 7th June – Last view of dear old Ireland, on the 2nd morn, deck rocks, writing stops. Severe headaches, violent pain. Stupefied, unable to fix eyes. Motion makes head giddy. Retire to ladies' part of cabin -2 wide berths; I, in one with maid and daughter. Room to stand and dress between. Two families, 19 persons here together in 1 space to sleep. Midnight - great swell, such a roll. Tumble over bed fellows. Trunks, boxes, baskets slide down leeside. Week 2: fine, sat on deck. Calm evening, sailors dance. In morrow's storm, confined to cabin and berth. Foggy, damp, cold. Midsummer temperature, 42° at Noon. Disheartening: state of feverish impatience to end voyage, be settled in our log home. Very cold, tormentingly calm, ten days little progress, constant tacking, tedious passage. July 4th, first sight of land in 33 days. Fine headlands, Cape Breton hills after Grand Banks. Pilot aboard, slowly up Gulph of St. Lawrence. Water, brown after dark blue Atlantic. July 13th: thick fog, narrow escape, large vessel nearly ran us down. July 14, morning, thick fog. Dreadful shock: strange, horrible sensation as if every piece of timber tearing. Ship struck rock, sticking fast. Tide ebbing, nothing known of damage nor of removal plan till tide-flow. Confusion & terror. Hold passengers, clamerous. Capt. prevailed with difficulty till damage ascertained. Lying close to small bare island with reefs, rocks stretching like starfish rays. Ship caught. Shallows; c'd see rock, pilot had mistaken location. People seen on island, shot heard. 4 men in Canoe, spoke different French, home from seal shoot, rather handsome, Mocasins, shoes of Deerskin. Continued in State of Suspense till tide enabled movement. Dreadful scrape, set sail. July 21st: Docked, Port of Quebec; passage of 7 weeks, 1 day. Free from cabin mates &118 hold settlers.

shark^

por
poise
pois por
por ise

Pestilence, Gros Isle

from:
The Backwoods of Canada,
Catharine Parr Traill,
Letter II, Aug. 6-9, 1832

Unfolding "Pestilence, Gros Isle"

Parr Traill must have been horrified by her inability to protect herself and her loved ones from exposure to cholera. Powerless to escape the disease either in her home port of Leith or in the new colony, her ship sailed up the Gulf of St. Lawrence, inching closer to disembarkation and actual physical confrontation with the threat. At Grosse Isle, Canada's version of Ellis Island, the letter-writer reported the visible evidence of that menace, poetically indicated by large bold type face, as she watched first the procession of both the ill and the healthy from the decks of a diseased transport and then, the indiscriminate scattering of each passenger's life possessions along the shoreline. Imagine the fear she experienced as she observed fumigation rituals, the fort, and the garrison of troops, all measures meant to protect but now proven to be ineffective in the containment of the illness. She had no choice but to proceed to her destination.

Pilot's pamphlet Board of Health, Quebec, regulations

respecting

cholera cholera cholera cholera cholera cholera

forbid any person, whether crew or passenger
quitting vessel until shall have passed an examination

quarantine ground detained there three days having sailed from infected port
Gros Isle several vessels lying at anchor
yellow flag melancholy symbol of disease

cholera cholera cholera cholera cholera cholera

invalids conveyed to cholera hospital

cholera cholera cholera cholera cholera cholera

hospital surrounded by palisades, guard of soldiers
fort garrison of troops, enforces quarantine rules,
produce severe evils to unfortunate emigrants, healthy but in vicinity of infection

cholera cholera cholera cholera cholera cholera

landed passengers from three emigrant ships
evidence of every variety of disease, vice, poverty, filth, famine
bedding, clothes spread out, washed, aired, fumigated
human misery most disgusting, saddening form

cholera cholera cholera cholera cholera cholera

fear

Pestilence, Montreal

from:
The Backwoods of Canada,
Catharine Parr Traill,
Letter III, Aug. 17, 1832 and
Roughing It in the Bush,
Susanna Moodie,
Chapter 4, "Our Journey up the
Country," 1832-33

Unfolding "Pestilence, Montreal"

Think of the mincing steps taken by the sisters, Parr Traill and Moodie, and their parties as they gingerly explored for the first time, a Canadian settlement beyond the deck. Their sense of freedom from confinement aboard ship was negated by the sights, sounds and smells of a city under siege. Cholera surrounded them and their panic knew no bounds. The number of the dead, x'd from life's roster, climbed alarmingly not only in the streets but also in the surrounding countryside and found a particularly hospitable welcome amongst their fellow passengers, debilitated from their extended crossing, the crowded conditions in the hold and by their diminished supplies. News that the plague might have spread to Upper Canada emphasized once again the inescapable hazards, cholera being just one of many, awaiting them as they proceeded inland. An ominous beginning to a new life …

cholera cholera cholera cholera cholera cholera

Montreal: city of pestilence, feeling of anxiety and dread
horror of infection increased as we sailed close,

Captain's history: left disease in Russia – found it in Leith – met it again in Canada
formerly calm now confided conviction should never quit city alive
third confrontation no escape

cholera cholera cholera cholera cholera cholera

dirty, narrow,
ill-paved or un-paved streets,
overpowered by the noisome
vapour
arising from a deep open fosse,
receptacle for every abomination,
sufficient in itself to infect the town

cholera cholera cholera cholera cholera cholera

opening of all its sewers,
long neglected uncleanliness,
to stop the ravages of the pestilence --
rendered the thoroughfares almost impassible --
loaded the air with intolerable effluvia

cholera cholera cholera cholera cholera cholera

hxndrxds of xmxgrxnts dix dxxly,
sullen txll of death bxll,
expxsure of ready-mxde cxffins in undxrtxkers' windxws
print placxrds of funerxls at chexpest rxte xnd at shxrt notxcx

cholera cholera cholera cholera cholera cholera

awful rxvxges,
dxvxstxtxng xffxtcs,
dxrkxnxd dwxllxngs,
mxxrnfxl hxbxlmxnts xf xll clxssxs,
dxjxctxxn xnd anxxxty xn xll fxcxs,
strxxts nxxrly dxpxpxlxtxd,
thxsx xlxvx flxd pxnxc-strxckxn
tx thxxr cxxntry vxllxgxs
tx dxx xn thx bxsxm xf thxxr fxmxlxxs –

cholera cholera cholera cholera cholera cholera

mxst fxtxlly xffxctxd –
pxxrxr xmxgrxnts,
dxbxlxtxtxd by prxvxtxxns
xnd fxtxgxx xf our 9 wxxk vxyxgx

cholera cholera cholera cholera cholera cholera

xn one hxxsx – 11 dxxd
anxthxr – 17,
chxld of 7 xlivx tx txll thx woxfxl txlx

cholera cholera cholera cholera cholera cholera

stories that the plague extends to Kingston

cholera cholera cholera cholera cholera cholera

Rapids Upriver

from:
Revisiting "Our Forest Home,"
The Immigrant Letters
of Frances Stewart,
Letter, late August, 1822

Unfolding "Rapids Upriver"

Poled by a team of French Canadians past Montreal, four bateaux carried the Stewart party of 19 westwards. Frances's account of this trek is encapsulated within boat-shaped word-rails which not only entrap the group in their discomfort but provide my own enhanced interpretation of the bare-bones experience she recorded. The pioneer-travellers were constricted not only by the river's tumultuous width, the wood-ribbed gunwales of their boats, their uncomfortable seating, their inability to communicate with their guides, and by the vagaries of weather but also by the narrow shoreline path, crowded between forest and rushing water, upon which they had to tread when the rapids became violent. There was no shade; there was no shelter; there were sometimes dreadful sleeping accommodations and unwelcoming hosts; there was no choice but to put one foot ahead of the other and to bear the discomfort and the fatigue with stoic fortitude. Frances wrote only the facts of this journey and was strangely reticent to reveal her feelings as though complaints were an unacceptable convention.

burning rays, backs ramrod straight, oppressive heat, no shade, breathless and humid glinting sun

glinting

In four open batteaux, perched uncomfortably on our luggage
for many of the next long 173 miles. Weather very hot, sun inescapable.
Slept at farm houses and stopped at cottages to procure bread & milk.
Violent rushing water over giant stones, a great contrast to the smooth
glassy breadth of the river heretofore. Hottest day during our lives.
Our boatmen, all French Canadian could not speak a word of English.
When Rapids were too violent & with the current against us, our boatmen stopped rowing
& took long poles to push the boats on. We unloaded to lighten the load and walked,
woman for five, but men and boys for twelve miles or more, with trunks

sun on running water, no support for aching backs, oppressive heat, no shade, no shelter glinting

sun burn, trudging pace, weight of sun on heads, heat rash, weary steps, boots that rub aching toes red

rash of red

and children in hired carts beside us. Progress very slow and painful
every step. Baby Bessy fevered & teething.
At the inn, accommodations were very bad; the beds were swarming with bugs,
so we spread mattrasses of our own on the floor but we could not bear
those bugs which crawled all over us & all over the walls & floors,
till we spread our cloaks over sweet smelling hay in the barn and were lulled by the water
sounds. Never was a bed of down so delightful.
We awoke at half-past three & were glad to lose a few hours of sleep that we might

peeling nose, itch to scratch, boots that rub, miles to trudge, bonnets tied too tight aching toe

bugs crawling, bugs climbing, bugs delving, bugs biting, welted bites, itching red bites swollen bug

burrowed

gain a few hours of coolness. We had a heavy shower midday that
drenched us completely even though we covered ourselves by
lying under the tarpaulins covering our luggage. Due to the high heat of the day,
there was no fire at the next cottage where we could dry
our dripping garments. Wet still, we returned to the batteaux
continuing upriver till midnight in our damp State.
Dried out at Charlottenburg, we renewed our tedious journey. The day
grew very stormy; we were wet through all our clothes. I was never so

bites beneath nightclothes, in armpits and secret spots, red bites, itching bites swollen swollen

rain dripping from nose, rain running down the face, wet hair dripping down the neck thunderous skies

soaked wet

wet in all
my life. Even under us was wet.
I never saw such awfully heavy rain or such cross people;
angry for us before the fire, they pushed us away and complained
of us and the noisy children dirtying the floor. Nearly dark but we had to
go a good way splashing through the puddles & wet to the next farmhouse.
Mattrass wet so I left it airing. Lay down without undressing in the barn where
there was plenty of clean straw.
Next day, a rapid which lasted for three miles.

lightning flashes, chaffing garments, wet leather boots squelching in muddy-grass, shivering

Rampant

from:
The Backwoods of Canada,
Catharine Parr Traill,
Letter VII and VIII, 1833.

Unfolding "Rampant"

In this poem, I wished to convey the sense of compression felt by the letter-writer when surrounded by the rampant growth of the forest and by the solitude and silence, uninterrupted except by the tapping of the woodpeckers, the rustling of the chipmunks and the soughing of the wind in the tall tree tops. When I first started to write, I ordered the piece from top to bottom but realized that a bottom-up progression might better reflect a mapped entry into the woods and the sort of staggered, winding pathway required by the many obstacles along the route. When night swiftly fell, the husband-wife pair found themselves lost in the wilderness. The husband back-tracked their route, looking for help and left Parr Traill, stiff with fright, alone in the dark. The title pinpoints that rampant stance, upright with fists raised to protect or to attack, as well as the courage required of settlers in facing a dread unknown.

hemlock, beech, white pine, white pine, maple, maple, fir, fir, fir, balsam, hemlock, hemlock, hemlock, maple
white pine, white pine, white pine, maple, maple, fir, fir, fir, balsam, hemlock, beech, beech, beech, maple, beech
maple, maple, fir, fir, fir, balsam, hemlock, hemlock, maple, maple, maple,   fir,
maple, fir, fir, fir, balsam, hemlock, hemlock, maple, maple,   fir,
fir, fir, balsam, hemlock, hemlock, hemlock, maple, maple, beech, fir,   hemlock,
white pine, white pine, maple, maple, fir   fir,
chipmunk, white pine, fir, pine, woodpecker   maple
white pine, maple, fir, balsam, beech,
chipmunk, jack pine, fir, maple, balsam,
maple, fir, beech
hemlock

wind in the tree tops
hoarse and mournful cadence

h a l l o o o o o

silence, solitude

no gleam of light
no sign of habitation
deepening darkness

t a p - t a p - t a p

mud holes
cedar swamp
mud holes

f a l l e n t r e e s

corduroy bridge
roots of trees
limestone boulders,
lumps of granite
corduroy bridge

ol
j t
o t
j l
o
j lt

c o r d u r o y b r i d g e

trunks and sundry packages
seat - carpet bags,
rough deal box on wheels
wagon -

blazes
no palpable road,

fir
pine,
fir
pine, fir
pine, beech,
fir, balsam, maple, beech
maple, beech, hemlock,
fir, fir, woodpecker, white pine
maple   fir   pine, pine, balsam, maple, beech,
white pine, white pine, maple, maple, fir, fir, fir, balsam, maple,
fir, fir, balsam, hemlock, hemlock, hemlock, maple, maple, beech, fir, hemlock
maple, fir, fir, fir, balsam, hemlock, hemlock, maple, maple, beech, beech, fir, maple,
maple, maple, fir, fir, fir, balsam, hemlock, hemlock, maple, maple, fir, jack pine, maple, hemlock, beech, beech, fir,
white pine, white pine, maple, maple, fir, fir, fir, balsam, hemlock, hemlock, maple, beech,
hemlock, beech, white pine, white pine, maple, maple, fir, fir, fir, balsam, hemlock, hemlock, maple, balsam, jack pine

Homestead

from:
Revisiting "Our Forest Home,"
The Immigrant Letters
of Frances Stewart,
Letter, Feb. 24th, 1823

Unfolding "Homestead"

In this poem, I wanted to contrast the delighted anticipation of the Stewart family at the prospect of finally reaching the new residence, after eight months of journeying and borrowed beds, and the reality of its unfinished and almost unlivable state upon arrival. The fire in the hearth, visually created here by the stacked stone hearth placement of the words, had thrown such a welcoming light that Frances had been initially encouraged by its glow through the trees. I wished, once again, to capture that sense of layered entrapment experienced by the young family between the extreme cold pressing on their unprotected flesh and the enveloping smoke, as they huddled uncomfortably on the rough floor-boards before that fire whose warmth was so quickly escaping through the uncompleted door openings. My bold black font encircles and compresses the tiny family, into a squashed and shivering state.

own
home
in view
at last,
must
bear
good deal of
inconvenience
for some time yet
while settling in,
first joy
I felt for
quite some
weary time
Douro Loghouse looks comfortable, happy,
cabin windows quite illuminated by glare in
distance of charming fires, such a delightful
anticipation at glad prospect of final arrival --

oh... oh ... oh...

COLD smoke COLD
COLD COLD house in very unfinished state **COLD COLD**
smoke COLD COLD doors everywhere not hung **COLD COLD smoke**
smoke COLD COLD upper part of chimney built of boards, **COLD COLD smoke**
smoke COLD COLD as frost made it impossible **COLD COLD smoke**
smoke COLD COLD to go on with mason work; **COLD COLD smoke**
smoke COLD COLD as it smokes, Tom's hasty & temporary repairs **COLD COLD smoke**
smoke COLD COLD must be rebuilt in spring **COLD COLD smoke**
smoke COLD COLD COLD COLD smoke
smoke COLD COLD first night very uncomfortable **COLD COLD smoke**
smoke COLD COLD eleven degrees below zero this morning **COLD COLD smoke**
smoke COLD COLD fire blazing since, both day and night **COLD COLD smoke**
smoke COLD COLD children and adults bedded on floors in single room **COLD COLD smoke**
smoke COLD COLD {close bundled before hearth} **COLD COLD smoke**
smoke COLD COLD COLD COLD smoke

Bitter Trial, Days 1-3

from:
Revisiting "Our Forest Home,"
The Immigrant Letters
of Frances Stewart,
Letter, Oct. 1823

Unfolding "Bitter Trial, Days 1-3"

Poor wee Bessy: child of two years and third born of Frances' eventual 11 offspring, she managed to survive the long ocean voyage, the claustrophobic bateau trip past the rapids, the freezing winter journey north to the property, the bitter early time in an unfinished cabin and the intervening months of heat and swamp fevers. In October, she was stricken with dysentery and her mother found herself without either the resources or the knowledge to fight the illness. Helpless and panic-stricken, the letter-writer had nothing to relieve the enfeebled state of her dying child; she was still grieving the child's loss six years later when she wrote her "Elegy on Little Bessy." In my poem, I envisioned the stacked verses of the elegy as the tiny pine box of the baby's burial, and the specifics of her tragic final days as the wooden cross marking the resting place of her wasted body.

Douro
fall
arrival
Baby
dysentery.
Ignorant of
disease, no doctor within reach, nearest
many miles distant. No canoe; hired man
swam river & walked to fetch
powders
advice.
Sick and
feeble,
child
refused
Arrowroot;
craved
bread but
no flour…
Near
midnight,

fell into stupor.

Angel spirit passed to immortal land on 20/10/23

Elegy on Little Bessy (Elizabeth Augusta Stewart) 1821-1823. from: *The Commonplace Book of Frances Stewart,* 1829, Trent University Archives.

Soft is thy Thunder, infant child, / And still thy tranquil sleep.
Unheard by thee the Tempest wild / That o'er thy tomb may sweep.

No Marble now marks thy lowly grave
No stone thy modest tomb
But Hemlocks wild o'er thee doth wave.
With branch of Sombre gloom.

What though the soil unhallowed be
That marks thy sad decay
Thy sleep is soft beneath that tree
On shady Hemlock Brae.

Stranger, if there thou chance to stray
To Bessy's tomb … stay
A while thy wandering footsteps
Nor check the rising tear.

Bitter Trial, Day 4

from:
Revisiting "Our Forest Home," The Immigrant Letters of Frances Stewart,
Letter, Oct. 1823

Unfolding "Bitter Trial, Day 4"

If losing a child was not enough, the process of burial was even harder for Frances especially when the child had to be laid to rest in the inhospitable rocky outcropping of the Canadian Shield. The letter-writer's description of the burial is heart-rending. The entire community, 27 souls, attended the service, the first observance of the Church of England prayers in this remote area. The small size of the grave was diminished further by the height of the trees and the vastness of the forest stretching in all directions, ultimately compressing Bessy's brief life and tragic death to a mere footnote of history and swallowing whole her mother's grief. The drear location, although sheltered by the hemlock branches, is disturbing for the trees are huge, tough, dark and gray; their shade is somber and solemn while the enveloping silence is eerily mournful, rendering spectator sorrow into a sort of breathless misery.

Assembly:
whole settlement,
27 souls

only Christian inhabitants
in v - a – s - t
forest

s t r e t c h i n g
thousands
miles
unbroken
east and north
of Otonabee
& little Lake,

grave
youngest
most endearing
little band of Pilgrims

arrived
last year
at Port of Quebec

resting place
lay
sloping ground
known
Hemlock Bray
beneath
four [ ] hemlock
pines

spreading
branches
found
a perfect canopy

whose huge…
tough…
dark…
gray…
trunks
& stems

spiral tops
towered
far above

carrying
hearts, eyes
far away
clear vault of heaven.

no human architect
could equal
grandeur
solemn

somber shade
sorrowing group

mournful silence

strong and hardy
breathless

knowing
solitude

powerless
restrain
outpouring

deep memory
swelling heart
joined

first time
Church of England
burial service

midst
little
band
Pioneers
founded settlement
vast wilderness.

hallowed spot

heartfelt prayer

little Bessie,
laid
beneath
noble
Hemlock trees.

Settling Bee

from:
The Backwoods of Canada,
Catharine Parr Traill,
Letters VIII and IX,
The Lake House, April 18, 1833

Unfolding "Settling Bee"

In this poem, the vertical and horizontal text represents the hand-hewn floorboards, the chopped log walls and the chinking compressed into the open spaces between; the wood was uneven in width and length, un-planed, and full of splinters. Onto this rough foundational expanse and into this dark, confining and unfinished space the family settled, happy to have a roof as shelter from wintery gales, for it was by then November. The letter-writer was grateful, despite the log home's gloomy space, for her family was better off than others of the community. That so few comforts, after so many frustrations and delays, could offer them such relative ease of mind was a testament to the couple's willingness to suffer much for the long-term possibilities that they might wrest from the wilderness, however bleak their current prospects.

adze saw knots axe
oxe sleepers saws
floors logs floors log

3 acres ready for spring crops: oats, pump-
kins, Indian corn, potatoes - planted around
the stumps which take 7 - 9 years to decay -

loss of yoke of oxen bought to draw logs from
woods to cabin site – 1 of unlooked for delays
– forded lake, marched off leaving no trace,

chinkchi
nkchink
chinkchi
nkchink

missing 1 month,
located twenty
miles away at

logs hands home of former owner, oxen moved past bush, through mud, swamp, creek & lake where man would not go; on un-

delays
delays
delays
delays

favourable day, 16 neighbours raised
outer walls with Canadian "nectar,"
joint of salt pork, peck of potatoes, rice

p u d d i n g ;
little appearance of a house, oblong square, open spaces between
logs, doors and windows not chopped out, rafters not up, a queer

p l a c e ;
later - sleepers laid to
support floors and win-

dows, doors cut from solid timbers; floor boards had to be sawn
by hand in absence of mill, high wages; man injured leg with

carelessness, whole process delayed until healed; timber unseasoned,
could not be planed, must accept rough appearance, slivers until sum-

mer, when
house will

ch
in
kc
hi
n
kc
hi
n
kc

be topsy-turvy, floors re- laid,
jointed, smoothed; next, roof shin-
gled; 3rd misfortune, mix of lime
and clay to plaster inside and be-

tween chinks of logs was one night frozen to stone when work half completed, proceedings put to stop as
plaster yielded neither to fire nor to hot water, the latter freezing before it had an effect. 2nd man injured
from axe blade when smoothing; result - a very humble dwelling; husband becomes glazier with boxes of
glass of different sizes at a cheap rate to prepare frame before fixing it in, only a part of original plan finished,

smoothing injuries delays not chopped for-
mer oxen careless rough broken nectar

- rest must be added later as circumstances allow; most crockery broken in
short, rough journey through woods but we are now left with small sitting

adze broken
oxe yoke ford
gone 20 days
chink chink
chink freezing
nights weather
injuries delays

room & store closet, kitchen with pantry and bedchamber on our
ground floor, a good upper floor that will make 3 sleeping spaces;
this is currently our nut shell only until we add our bedding, boxes,

trunks & other possessions; such dire and extremely lengthy
difficulties we encountered seeing the fulfillment of our plans
but the greatest satisfaction to see few better off than we …

Snow Socked

from:
Revisiting "Our Forest Home,"
The Immigrant Letters
of Frances Stewart,
Letters, Jan. 27 and Feb. 5, 1824

Unfolding "Snow Socked"

The harsh realities of everyday life in the wilderness must have been shocking to the newcomers. Frances Stewart's description of her husband's life-threatening struggle while travelling home from Cobourg, provide the modern reader insight into the perilous existence with which our forebears were all too familiar. His survival on lake ice, shoreline indecipherable, enveloped by snow, in wet and freezing attire was questionable and the result of great good fortune. How minute he was in the immense white landscape while flakes of snow intruded on his thoughts and wind squalls blocked out portions of his words. My snowflakes, in this poem, attempt to re-create in type the same effect, nearly blotting out the man, his life story and almost the entire visible spectrum of his surroundings.

**
To Cobourg by the New road: * *
Husband Tom found tedious the trip, * *
in *coach sleigh drawn by oxen, * *
** whole day * to travel 9 miles * *
* *
overnight, slept at an ** old highlander, * * *
** husband * of my femme sage, * *
proceeded * alone in borrowed sleigh, * *
* *reached Cobourg safely * *
returning, * * * *
* * crossed iced * Rice Lake, * *
in* highlander*s * sleigh; * * * *
* * ** ** waited & walked ** shoreline *
*
till coach sleigh * would c*me up, * * * *
* * * **long time* in sn*w * * * *
* * * back* tracked* *ver lake * * * * * * * * * *
** * * * listen*ng * for appr*ach *of conveyance, * * *
* * * * *** * * sudden * *thick**sn*w **sh*wer*s * * * *
* * acc*mpi*d by *strong wind* ** * * * * * * *
*land n*t visibl*e* * * * * ** * * * * ** * * *
* n* s*und by which t* st**r * his c*urse* * * * * * * * ** * * **
* * * ** ti*d d*wn e*rs of cap, *butt*n*d *c*at *tight* *** * * ** * * * ** * ** * * * * **
** ** * * * *****tri*d*t* g*ain *ne*ar-by isl*nd* ** * * * * *
* *** * ** ********lost direc*ti*n, *sh*rli**ne, * invisi*b*le* * * ** * * ** * *
** *** * ******** * *** ** ** ** ** * ***** ***
* ** **** * ** ***** **** *** * **** ** *** **** *** ***
****
_____*** *_________* *________***** * **_____* __***_*****______***_
* * *surr*und*ed*by atm*sphr*ere* *f *Wind* *& *sn*w ** * *** * * * * * * * ***
****** * m*ost *intense**ly *c*ld,*t** *c* ld *for** plea*sure, * * *** * ** *** ****
unc*rta**ble * si*tua*tion,** c*onsi*deri*ng **p*ros*pects* * * *** ***** *** ** *****
** * ** *** ** ** ****
**** * **** h**eard** s*me*one**c*all*&* an*swer*ed * ** *** ***** *** ** * *
** * *
* ** *****C*ome** h*me *with** me to *Anders*n*s H*use** * * ** *** ** * **
*or**you *shall* **sure*ly* per**ish*** ** *** ** ** *** * *** * *** ***** **
* ** * * * **** *** *** ****************** * * * * * *
** *** Kin*d*&* Hospi*table;**** Tom's Equipage*** *arriv*ed***** * ** ** *** *** * *
****** * H*me**safe & * Heart*ily tired** * * *** *** **
*** ***** ***** **of the**xen Sleigh** & * new r*ad, *** * *** ** * * *** * ** ***
**** ** ** *** * **** ** *** ***** *** * * ** * * * ** * ** * * * ** * ****
** * *** **** **** *** * * ** * * * ** * ** * * * ** ****
**** ** *** **** *** *** ****************** * * **** *** * **** ** *** ****
* * *** ***
**** **** *** * **** ** *** **** *** ***

Threading A Maze

from:
Revisiting "Our Forest Home"
The Immigrant Letters of
Frances Stewart
Letter, May 27, 1826

Unfolding
"Threading A Maze"

Lack of ready money was a constant concern for the settler communities for not everything could be gleaned from their small cleared plots of land or from the animals for which they had bartered or exchanged their small store of cash. Credit at the distant grocer's was only briefly available and depended on repayment of previous loans. Frances was besieged by doubts, wondering in hindsight if the decision to immigrate had been the correct option for her family. As their fortunes fluctuated wildly with the years with no observable upward progress, she regretted her passivity in placing the choice entirely in her husband's hands. The phrases of this poem are surrounded by question marks and, like a pieced quilt, are sewn together by thread, in a random running stitch, as I try to replicate the racing mind of the letter-writer and to reflect the multitude of concerns, both large and small, that occupy her battling thoughts.

regrets doubts regrets

this kind of farming **doubts** regrets never profitable

for husband as gentleman regrets can never work nor can it be for children

?

would do better on small farm ??? doubts Tom, return home in a few years ?

? ? ?

prevented by fear from consulting regrets thinking and pondering, giving pain

no creature to talk to doubts too much to bear

? ???

continue as going regrets live to extent of income . . . .

?without much comfort ? ? seeing our children vulgar and illiterate?

? doubts ?

remove regrets to town as advised to do? . . . .

Peterboro little gossiping village . . . .

husband - sink into indolence, lose health doubts ? expense of building and purchasing

?? ???

Cobourg resettlement? regrets ?fresh expenses . . .

Society better doubts purchase and furnish house but still far from Irish friends

regrets ?

??income small doubts good management, small scale life means equal comfort as in cabin

????????

burden on friends/family regrets best reason for not returning to Ireland . . . . .

taken advice, in hindsight ? avoided emigrating so hastily . . . . . .

I argued/entreated doubts his mind bent on it, my duty was to yield**??**

right to come here regrets never happy had he not done so **??**

? ?

rented cleared farm ??? doubts would have done well, no disappointment, hardship,

?? ?? children gentle in manners and minds improved **???**

regrets **???**

separate from Reid family **? ? ?** doubts for them, woods were best

no use in useless regrets regrets kindness to brother in law was good motive **?**

regrets doubts

?? prospect of succeeding here ??? doubts w'ld rather live in small way near friends than here

where if desirous of advice must wait a half year to receive it . . .

regrets ???

???better to persevere here or openly encourage him to stop ?? ?

doubts

in many little dilemmas ? ? ? regrets **would give anything for a friend to consult**

doubts regrets **doubts** **regrets** doubts

The Unnaturals

from:
Roughing It in the Bush,
Susanna Moodie
Chapter 4, "The Charivari,"
undated

Unfolding "The Unnaturals"

This poem evolved from my impression that there were certain segments of the pioneer community which lived shadowy and peripheral existences, ostracized because of their willingness to engage in an alternate life-style. I chose to box these folk in, place them far from the core of my page and to paint their lives in contrary white font. Connecting them to the settlement at large are imagined silken threads forming a web at whose centre, crouching menacingly in large bold font like a giant black spider, are the unruly and ungovernable mob voices. Under the cover of dark, that suppressed fury at those making daring choices erupted into savagery and the protesters moved from grumbling intolerance to outright and unpunished harassment and murder.

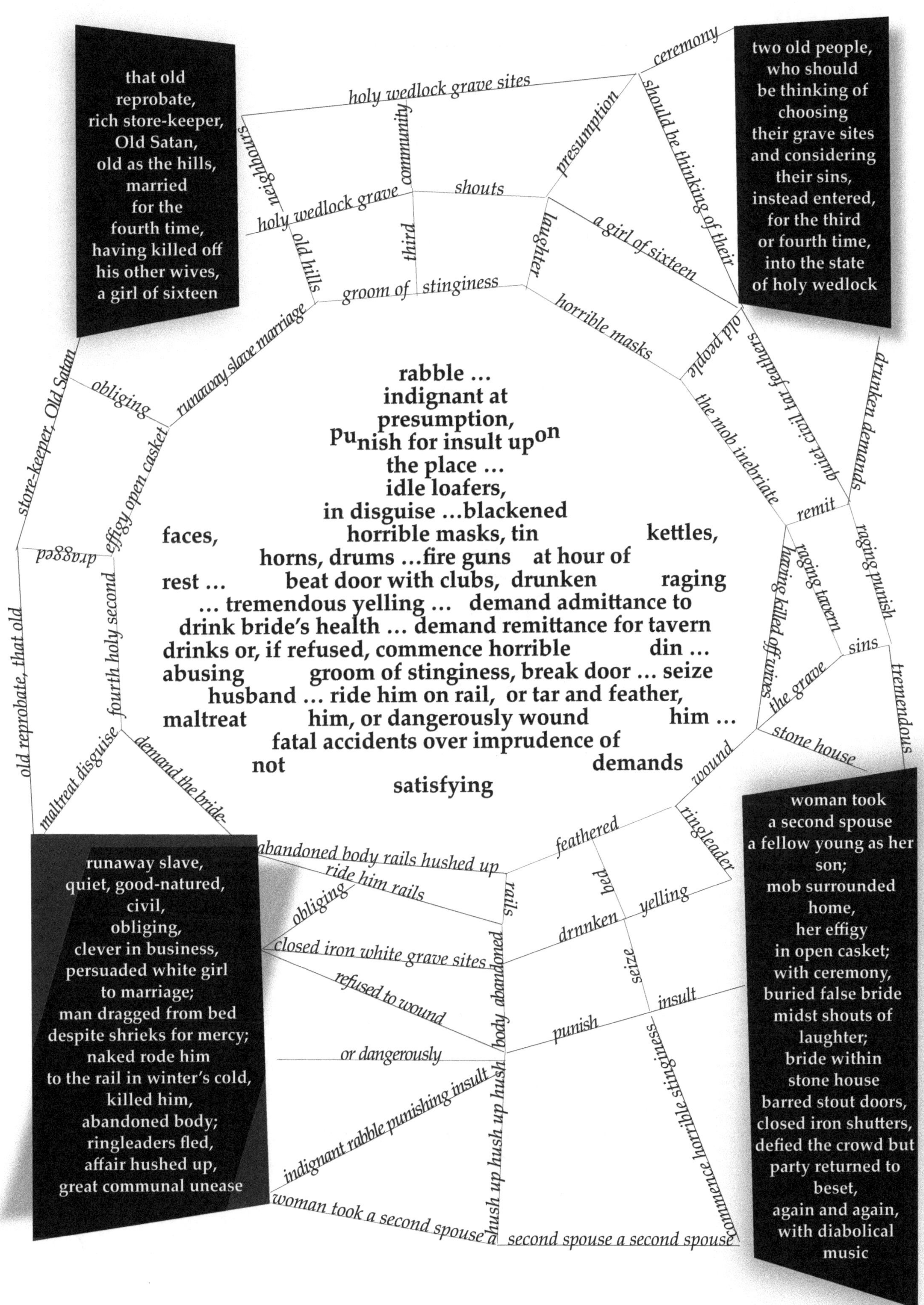
that old
reprobate,
rich store-keeper,
Old Satan,
old as the hills,
married
for the
fourth time,
having killed off
his other wives,
a girl of sixteen
two old people,
who should
be thinking of
choosing
their grave sites
and considering
their sins,
instead entered,
for the third
or fourth time,
into the state
of holy wedlock
rabble …
indignant at
presumption,
punish for insult upon
the place …
idle loafers,
in disguise …blackened
faces, horrible masks, tin kettles,
horns, drums …fire guns at hour of
rest … beat door with clubs, drunken raging
… tremendous yelling … demand admittance to
drink bride's health … demand remittance for tavern
drinks or, if refused, commence horrible din …
abusing groom of stinginess, break door … seize
husband … ride him on rail, or tar and feather,
maltreat him, or dangerously wound him …
fatal accidents over imprudence of
not demands
satisfying
runaway slave,
quiet, good-natured,
civil,
obliging,
clever in business,
persuaded white girl
to marriage;
man dragged from bed
despite shrieks for mercy;
naked rode him
to the rail in winter's cold,
killed him,
abandoned body;
ringleaders fled,
affair hushed up,
great communal unease
woman took
a second spouse
a fellow young as her
son;
mob surrounded
home,
her effigy
in open casket;
with ceremony,
buried false bride
midst shouts of
laughter;
bride within
stone house
barred stout doors,
closed iron shutters,
defied the crowd but
party returned to
beset,
again and again,
with diabolical
music
holy wedlock grave sites
ceremony
neighbours
community
presumption
should be thinking of their
holy wedlock grave
shouts
old hills
third
laughter
a girl of sixteen
groom of
stinginess
horrible masks
old people
quiet civil tar feathers
drunken demands
store-keeper, Old Satan
obliging
runaway slave marriage
the mob inebriate
effigy open casket
remit
dragged
raging punish
raging tavern
having killed off wives
fourth holy second
old reprobate, that old
sins
tremendous
the grave
stone house
maltreat disguise
demand the bride-
wound
ringleader
feathered
abandoned body rails hushed up
ride him rails
rails
bed
obliging
drnnken
yelling
closed iron white grave sites
seize
refused to wound
body abandoned
insult
punish
or dangerously
indignant rabble punishing insult
hush up hush up hush
commence horrible stinginess
woman took a second spouse a
second spouse a second spouse

Ring of Fire

from:
Roughing It in the Bush,
Susanna Moodie,
Chapter 17, "Burning the Fallow,"
Late summer, 1834

Unfolding "Ring of Fire"

The bold type of this poem surrounds and almost suffocates the small interior cabin, suggesting the seriousness of the fire's threat to the residents. The small fine type inside the small home indicates both the trapped family's insignificance as opposed to the unrestrained power of the blaze and its inability either to survive the flames or to escape the cage of log walls. Moodie's description of the intensity of the heat, the roar of the flames and the speed with which the fire moved to cut the family off from rescue is frightening for any empathetic reader. The closely packed words and the breathless quality of the lengthy single sentence of my poem are meant to evoke that sense of panic and confusion that Moodie felt as she attempted to problem-solve an escape route when there was none available to her little family. I created the midnight dreamscape at the poem's conclusion from varieties of trees, named throughout the book. These would have grown about the Moodie woodlot and probably would have inhabited her sleep scenes.

after late cold spring, burning hot summer, the hottest I ever remember;
no rain for many weeks till nature drooped and withered beneath one bright blaze of sunlight;
confusion of uncleared brush and fallow, spread littered around on every side; husband called away
on business with instructions not to burn until his return but hired help fell sick with ague and returned to own home leaving behind one
young obstinate lad; day sultry with strong wind at noon that roared in the pine tops like the dashing of distant bellows; heat unabated;
what a smoke! at door, nothing distinguishable beyond ten feet; cedar swamp on fire; wind driving dense black cloud;
lad had set fire in fifty places; horror, surrounded, wall of ash flames, cut off from all retreat, no one to discover
situation, beyond reach of aid; stupefied by helplessness; arc tears, lamentations useless; horrible death impending;
smoke canopy appalling; red forks of lurid flame floating safety smoke as tall as the tree tops, igniting them; crackling &
roaring; deep gloom blotted out the heavens, ash two angels, swirls mimics hell; birds' scorched wings,
resinous smell; parched with thirst, dear children in no drop of water in the house;
hissing flames gaining on us; thirst, sleep's embrace locked scorching breath on our faces; bitter
thought of husband's return the morrow; wind tight while blaze surrounds embers winds rise to hurricane
strength; scatter flames gusts house - untouched to foaming, scarlet, tidal waves;
terrific crash above of by devastation of fiery loud thunder; a breaking
waterspout of rain; ravenous maw of rushing silver torrent of
wet pent up ash the beast, airless particles these many weeks;
chip-yard was too soon afloat with gray ash,
embers and particulates; floating ash storm, unnoticed, had been
gathering all day and continued to rage all night and quite
subdued the dreadful cruel enemy; sank to our knees, lifted up our hearts in humble thanksgiving to God who had saved us by
an act of Providence from an awful and sudden death; from across the river, an unknown had spied the flames & had brought his canoe
to our landing but was too late to help us in our plight; husband listened to our tale with pale and disturbed countenance, not a little thankful to find
wife and offspring still in the land of the living; long after that day, fire haunted my dreams and I would awaken with a start,
fighting again the blaze, carrying children to location of safety where our garments, strangely, still
caught fire in that calm green clearing surrounded by maple, fir, poplar, cedar, scorch, hemlock, maple, birch,
hemlock, cedar, pine, hemlock, fir, balsam, scorch, maple, birch, hemlock, white pine, jack pine, maple, scorch, cedar

Desperation

from:
Roughing It in the Bush,
Susanna Moodie,
Chapter 21 and 24,
"Disappointed Hopes,"
1836-37

Unfolding "Desperation"

The recession of 1836-37, felt around the world, created extreme difficulties for Moodie's family. As each successive disaster, in large bold font, imperiled them the husband and wife staggered backwards disjointedly, to an unjustified right margin in my poem, in unconventional and constricted ways. At last, the dinner table was graced by weeds, boiled or served fresh, a crust or two of unappetizing bread from sprouted wheat, what could be salvaged from rotting potatoes, supplemented by the occasional fish or squirrel roast. Without hired help in the fields, future crop yields were compromised so that eventual bankruptcy was inevitable. In the midst of this penury, Moodie gave birth to her fourth child but her recovery was enfeebled by the want of fresh food. In an unforgiving and threatening landscape, the thin soil so far north of Lake Ontario not enriched by the silt of glacial melt, she and her family clutched desperately to an exposed and tiny plot of land.

wheat crop	lost to floods of rain
saved	barely enough to supply bad, sticky bread
debt	to pay our hired help
became field-labour	as ready money exhausted
steam boat speculation	reaped not a farthing
superfluities in groceries	given up
sustenance	produce of farm
milk, bread, potatoes	often only fare
sage and peppermint tea	herb at breakfast and tea time
root of the dandelion	beverage substitute when dried and ground
dandelion leaves	raw as salad, boiled as cabbage, fermented as beer
squirrel traps	supplied pies, stews and roasts
chissmunk	even palatable
lake, "Mama's Pantry"	bass and muskinongé
fine young bull	stolen by neighbor
pleadingly reclaimed	perpetrator, vengeful, drove six fat hogs into lake
grown flour, frosted potatoes, no meat	rendered us weak
weakened children	sick from the ague
deer flesh, good broth	restored sick to health for brief time
Katie's pet pig	sacrificed to butchering blade
hard times for second year	second son born
under-fed cows	not calved
dinner fare	consisted of soft rotting potatoes and still worse bread
malnourished nursing mother	spouse borrowed quarter mutton to rescue health
good faithful servant, sharing our tortures	obliged to leave
wage settlement	irreplaceable articles from wardrobe
ragged clothes	re-made for children

!!!Panic!!!
!!!Panic ... Panic... How to continue? Panic ...Panic ...!!!

Now, Fortune, do thy worst! For many years,
Thou, with relentless and unsparing hand,
Hast sternly pour'd on our devoted hearts
The poison'd phials of thy fiercest wrath.

!!!!!PANIC ... PANIC ... PANIC ... PANIC ... PANIC ... PANIC ... PANIC... !!!!!

Emblazoned

from:
Roughing It in the Bush,
Susanna Moodie
Chapter 23, "Fire,"
February 1837

Unfolding "Emblazoned"

After two years of desperate struggle to survive the recession, Moodie was subjected to the terrors of a second fire, her husband again from home. In this latest blow to fortune, the fright was even more dramatic as the winter conditions made it almost impossible to control the flames alone. In my imagination, I thought of Moodie as being almost walled in by the snow beneath her feet, freezing temperatures and icy lake winds buffeting her flanks while smoke, ash and embers from the burning rafters, shingles and chimney above blanketed her in a cloud. Helpless to cool the heat of the stove pipes, she was even more incapacitated in her efforts to reach the roof with either water or snow to smother the spreading flames. There were but two options: to evacuate what she was able to save and to preserve the lives of her babies. Her herculean efforts were fed by adrenalin and assisted only by the childish strength of her five year old daughter. Yet, the dreadful experience was emblazoned on the landscape, on the Moodie life-style choices as their few food stores had been destroyed, on the remnants of the loft areas, on her sleep patterns and on Susanna's health, so weak after child birth.

1837- severe winter, -18 to -27° … all liquids in house froze … husband from home … stove loaded with cedar chips for wood was green and set alight by naïve serving girl … crackling, roaring, smell of burned soot … stove/pipes red hot, blankets immersed in water wrapped around to cool … roof aflame, smoking, yesterday's deep snow all melted, shingles ignited … as ladder was at barn near road, stood on chair on table to throw up water then snow … sent girl for help, left alone with 4 children under 5 … Agnes, Dunbar and baby Daniel filled air with their cries, sheltered children under dresser until absolutely necessary to remove them for direful cold as bad as leaving them to mercy of fire … daughter Katie and I dragged bedding, clothing, trunks, boxes uphill, then dragged empty drawers far away, padded them with blankets … wrapped children in bedclothes, placing baby between knees of young Agnes, directing her to keep him well-covered … brisk breeze blowing up from lake fanned flames … roof now burning like brush-heap … we were working under burning shelf on which gun powder had been placed … child and I not able to make many more trips for goods … Katie saw father's flute, "Do save it; Papa will be sorry to lose it." God bless the dear child! … ah, how long help seemed in coming!

looked up, despairing, at road, saw man with others in distance, help at hand at last … had not felt cold, no cap, bonnet, no shawl, hands bare - now that help was close, knees trembled, felt giddy, faint, dark shadows dancing before eyes … husband sprang to burning loft and called for water but there was none left so that we lifted pails full of cold snow; filling them with frozen

hands was bitter work, work …the ladder was carried down… the burn-
ing roof was cut a cut away and flung into deep
banks of snow … brine from pickling beef checked
the fire's spread, Katie alone suffered from the intense
cold but for Katie … the poor creature's feet severely frozen and were snow-
rubbed … fire was extinguished before walls destroyed … loss of potatoes/flour …
fright and exertion left health in shock … new strength took time …

Sickness, Remedy, Quackery

from:
Roughing It in the Bush,
Susanna Moodie,
Chapter 4, "Our Journey Up the Country," 1832;
The Backwoods of Canada, Catharine Parr Traill,
Letter XVII, Nov. 18, 1834 and
Revisiting "Our Forest Home,"
The Immigrant Letters of
Frances Stewart,
Letter Sept. 21st, 1847

Unfolding "Sickness, Remedy, Quackery"

This trio of poems "Cholera," "Swamp Fevers" and "Typhoid," composed in crazy titling type face and with spinning circles, is my vision of the discombobulation which results when a loved one becomes ill. The whole house is thrown off-kilter as parties rally to resolve the problem. In pioneer times, that sense of intense disorientation was compounded by the dearth of medical care, the absence of medicines and the knowledge that death was an all too common fact of everyday life. Wives and mothers, in desperation, would have tried any remedy known, learned at mothers' knee or suggested, to save the person struck down with the mysterious ailment. The usual methods proving ineffective, concoctions made from ground roots, leaves, bark and twigs from the native peoples would have been implemented. The more serious or longer lasting the illness, the greater the sense of being powerless and the greater the effort to restore equilibrium in a topsy-turvy world or to step off, as in the case of my poems, the whirling platforms of the merry-go-round …

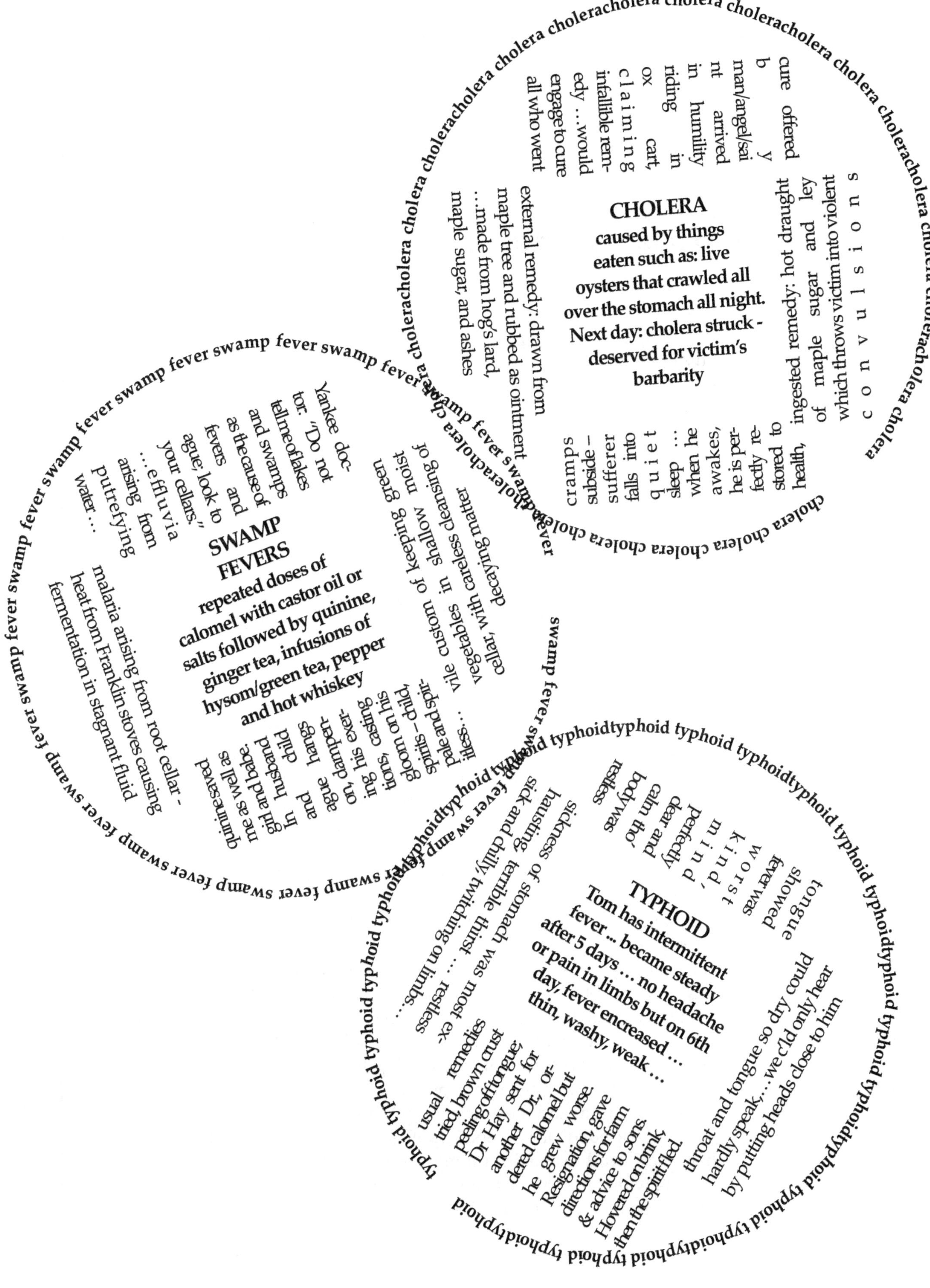

cholera choleracholera cholera choleracholera cholera choleracholera cholera cholera choleracholera cholera choleracholera cholera choleracholera cholera choleracholera cholera cholera cholera choleracholera cholera cholera
CHOLERA
caused by things eaten such as: live oysters that crawled all over the stomach all night. Next day: cholera struck - deserved for victim's barbarity
cure offered by man/angel/saint arrived in humility riding in ox cart, claiming infallible remedy …would engage to cure all who went
external remedy: drawn from maple tree and rubbed as ointment …made from hog's lard, maple sugar, and ashes
ingested remedy: hot draught of maple sugar and ley which throws victim into violent convulsions
cramps subside – sufferer falls into quiet sleep … when he awakes, he is perfectly restored to health,
swamp fever swamp fever swamp fever swamp fever swamp fever swamp fever swamp fever swamp fever swamp fever swamp fever swamp fever swamp fever swamp fever swamp fever swamp fever swamp fever
SWAMP FEVERS
repeated doses of calomel with castor oil or salts followed by quinine, infusions of ginger tea, pepper hysom/green tea, and hot whiskey
Yankee doctor: "Do not tell me of lakes and swamps as the cause of fevers and ague; look to your cellars." … effluvia arising from putrefying water …
vile custom of keeping green vegetables in shallow moist cellar, with careless cleansing of decaying matter
malaria arising from root cellar - heat from Franklin stoves causing fermentation in stagnant fluid
quinine saved me as well as girl and babe. In husband and child ague hangs on, dampening his exertions, casting gloom on his spirits – child, pale and spiritless…
typhoid typhoidtyphoid typhoid typhoidtyphoid typhoid typhoidtyphoid typhoid typhoid typhoidtyphoid typhoid typhoid typhoidtyphoid typhoid typhoid typhoidtyphoid typhoid typhoid typhoid
TYPHOID
Tom has intermittent fever ... became steady after 5 days … no headache or pain in limbs but on 6th day, fever encreased … thin, washy, weak …
tongue showed fever was worst kind, mind perfectly dear and calm tho' body was restless
sickness of stomach was most exhausting, terrible thirst … restless sick and chilly, twitching on limbs…
usual remedies tried, brown crust peeling off tongue, Dr Hay sent for another Dr, ordered calomel but he grew worse. Resignation, gave directions for farm & advice to sons. Hovered on brink then the spirit fled.
throat and tongue so dry could hardly speak,…we c'ld only hear by putting heads close to him

Oc Hone! Oc Hone!

from:
Roughing it in the Bush,
Susannah Moodie,
Chapter 24, "The Outbreak,"
undated

Unfolding
"Oc Hone! Oc Hone!'

I composed this poem as a ballad with the refrains offered by the Scottish serving woman's "oc hone, oc hone," as its first, and Moodie's own lament, "with a heavy heart," as its second. Research indicates that the rebellion referenced was that led in 1847-48 by William Lyon MacKenzie against the strict rule of the Family Compact, with support offered to the insurgents by invading American citizens. Rallied by broad sheets from Queen Victoria, backwoods settlers flocked to Toronto but were quickly dispersed, supplies being inadequate. However, the need for a standing militia to maintain control required that Susanna's husband be posted to the capital for a longer term. In the relative calm of backcountry pioneer life, the news of rebellion and invasion raised alarm bells and panic, indicated in this piece by the bold large type, the multitude of exclamation marks and by my image of old Jenny repeatedly wringing her hands and exclaiming "oc hone, oc hone." Alone but for her Scottish woman, Moodie was again intrepid, keeping together the dregs of her farm and the affections of her wee ones, ensuring the adequacy of food supplies, suppressing signs of her lonely heart to avoid alarming her offspring while still finding within herself the energy and resolve to obtain a small cash reserve with her nightly writing.

oc hone! oc hone!
long story from old Jenny
oc hone! oc hone!
some gentleman had called
during our absence
left a large paper

!!!Queen and the Yankees!!!
oc hone! oc hone!
!!!War!!!
!!!Canada and the States!!!
oc hone! oc hone!
!!!Toronto burnt!!!
!!!besieged by rebel force!!!
!!!Governor killed!!!
oc hone! oc hone!
!!!strange and monstrous statements!!!

once more safe by our fireside
elucidation of Jenny's marvellous tales

!!!Queen's proclamation!!!
oc hone! oc hone!
!!!all loyal gentlemen to join!!!
!!!putting down!!!
!!!unnatural rebellion!!!
oc hone! oc hone!

letter from sister, nature of outbreak
astonished settlers in the bush,
brother and sister's husband already joined
gentlemen collecting to march to aid Toronto
advised Moodie,
in weakened state,
oc hone! oc hone!
… stay home …

spirit of husband aroused
instantly obeyed imperative call of duty
ready to start the morrow
oc hone! oc hone!
little sleep, talked for hours …
coming separation,
might never meet again …
affairs in desperate condition
impossible to make worse
oc hone! oc hone!
to anxious wife, parting is finishing stroke
to misfortunes …
oc hone! oc hone!
cold, snowy morning broke …
children crying,
clinging to his knees …
too deeply affected to eat;
meal passed in silence
oc hone! oc hone!

put on hat and shawl
to accompany him through wood …
husband on crutches, we began our walk
oc hone! oc hone!
!!!day like our destiny!!!
!!!cold, dark and lowering!!!

oc hone! oc hone!
old Jenny's lamentations
oc hone! oc hone!
masther dear, why lave the wife and childher?
oc hone! oc hone!
poor crathur is breakin' her heart intirely at partin'
oc hone! oc hone!
shure an' the war is nothin' to you
that you must be goin' into danger – an' you wid a broken leg
oc hone! oc hone!
you will be kilt
oc hone! oc hone!
thin what will become of the wife and the wee bairns?
oc hone! oc hone!
lamentations followed us into the woods
oc hone! oc hone!

parted with a heavy heart …
with a heavy heart, retraced steps …
with a heavy heart, never felt bitter cold …
with a heavy heart, forgot all fears …
with a heavy heart, sad tears …
with a heavy heart, hope deserted me…
with a heavy heart, lay and wept …
with a heavy heart, all joy vanished …
with a heavy heart, absolute uncertainty as to the true state of affairs …
with a heavy heart, only conjectures; what might be the result …
with a heavy heart, listened to exaggerated accounts …

oc hone! oc hone!
!!!battle with rebels!!!
!!!defeat of loyalists!!!
!!!Toronto in state of siege!!!
!!!backwoods men ordered to march to relief of city!!!
oc hone! oc hone!
!!!battle with insurgents!!!
???Colonel Moodie, killed???
!!!rebels retreated!!!
???husband to return in few days???
!!!rebels were set of monsters!!!
oc hone! oc hone!
oc hone! oc hone!
!!!have no mercy!!!
!!!no punishment too severe!!!
oc hone! oc hone!

large force collected with rapidity …,
many half-pay officers,
experienced against armies of Napoleon …

our Moodie, home in one week …
too many volunteers …
no supplies to maintain them …
township companies remanded …
oc hone! oc hone!
!!!reunion brief!!!
!!!regiments of militia formed to defend!!!
!!!Moodie, given rank of captain!!!
!!!stationed in Toronto!!!
oc hone! oc hone!

long adieu …
with old Jenny and children,
looked after farm
oc hone! oc hone!
sad dull time,
gloom on my spirit …
oc hone! oc hone!

!!!full pay!!!
!!!signal act of mercy!!!
!!!liquidated pressing debts!!!
!!!procured few small comforts!!!
!!!shoes for the children!!!
!!!protection for little chapped feet!!!

but he was still long from home …
oc hone! oc hone!
occasional letter only solace …
oc hone! oc hone!
too poor to indulge often in such luxury …
oc hone! oc hone!

spring brought work …
borrowed sugar kettle to tap woods …
gathered and boiled sap, sugared off syrup …
gleaned 112 pounds of sugar, 6 gallons of molasses and 6 of vinegar …
potatoes and corn planted, garden cultivated, manure spread …
traded to drag a few acres of oats …
trapped eel, catfish in lake …
wrote by candlelight, realized $20.00 from editor …

oc hone! oc hone!
saddened by children's prattle of father
oc hone! oc hone!
daily walked with them through woods in vain hope of welcoming him
oc hone! oc hone!
oc hone! oc hone …

Bittersweet

from:
Roughing It in the Bush,
Susanna Moodie, Chapter 28,
"Adieu to the Woods,"
undated

Unfolding "Bittersweet"

Circumstances improved for the Moodie family thanks to the steady income from the father's militia service. However, debts were repaid in such small amounts and far too late for continued comfort while future prospects boded no radical change in fortune for them as harvests still promised to be scant. When an offer was presented to Moodie's husband for steady employment, the family was motivated to retire to a more propitious environment. Alone but for Jenny's assistance, Susanna disposed of their goods and packed up what was left for transport when the first snow fell to smooth the trail for sleigh travel. This poem traces the desperate conditions with which the Moodies had lived for a decade and a half and now must continue to endure till their departure and escape to town life. Note the incongruity of that china tea service found in their new home and its ironic contrast to the broken stove and the icicled food in their old. It is, however, a bittersweet moment for Susanna as the family had invested their all and had now so little to show for their sacrifices but for the dear friends who had sustained their spirits while suffering alongside them.

furious winter storms

wind blowing fiercely off lake, a lion roaring for its prey, shaking rafters,
driving snow through every open crevice of which there were not a few,
powdering floor until it rivalled in whiteness the ground without

broken stove around whose meager heat we huddled

dear forest home

loved in spite of its hardships
birthplace of three boys
school of high resolve in which we had learned

to meet calmly the ills of life

dawn

the whole forest scene lay glittering, a mantle of dazzling white,
cold so severe that every article of food had to be thawed before breakfast
blankets stiff with frozen breath; small windows half snow-blocked

scarce allowed a glimpse of declining sun

friends

oblivious to the cold, had waded forth to bid us farewell
silent, still thrust forth their hands in earnestness
true comrades to us

in our dire necessity

conflicting emotions

agitated severely my mind
looking for the last time upon that humble home
endeared to me in

a long exile from a civilised life

our holdings

lonely lake, belt of dark pines, cedar swamp
Otonobee, foaming, rushing, wildest and most beautiful of streams
snake-fenced garden where I laboured

braving tormenting mosquitoes, black flies and intense heat

then ...

a three day sleigh ride

hazardous with cold, a risk to the lives of the children
horses covered with icicles, hair frozen white
eyelids stiff, limbs aching with frost, teeth chattering

children crying with pain in fingers

in a distant town

met by him whom one and all so ardently longed to see
and were conducted to a pretty cottage
lovingly prepared

for our reception

old Jenny

guided me through the unfamiliar rooms
showed me furniture new-purchased
especially recommending to my notice

a china tea service

said

"Och! Who would have thought, misthress,
that we would be living in a mansion like this
and ating off real chaney when but yesterday

we were hoeing praties in the field."

Adieu! – adieu – when quivering lips refuse
The bitter pangs of parting to declare;
And the full bosom feels that it must lose
Friends who were wont its inmost thoughts to share ...

Weeds

from:
Revisiting "Our Forest Home,"
The Immigrant Letters of
Frances Stewart,
Letters to Ireland, friends and family,
Sept. 1847 - Jan., 1872

Unfolding "Weeds"

Interspersed among the verses of this dirge are the rules of mourning etiquette from a later era; their stipulations were as restricting as the lives and circumstances of the widows themselves. Not all pioneer women had the resilience of Moodie; some were flattened by adversity. The letters of Frances Stewart written from her husband's death in 1847 to her own death in1872, revealed not only a over-abundance of lamentations as she bemoaned her fate (and that of other women hobbled by the strict rule of their husbands) but also repeated evidence of a narrowing existence for her. At first, the widow shared her home, Auburn, with her son William, reserving a room or two for her own use and hoping that he would arise to the challenge and assume responsibility for residence and farm whose maintenance was beyond her. When he married, Frances found accommodation in a nearby rented home, into whose rooms she welcomed her widowed daughter and her children. Auburn, the prize earned by so much toil over a quarter of a century, was lost to the family through fraudulent dealings. Five sons neglected their mother, visiting seldom and rarely fulfilling her aspirations for them. Five daughters seemed to exhibit greater degrees of affection but were still a constant draw on Frances' slender means. Financially caged, Frances could rarely gift her grandchildren with other than written wishes. Finally, her world was even more restricted by rheumatism, deafness and loss of vision and by the passing of friends with whom she had corresponded for fifty years. Constantly mournful and self-deprecatory, dressed in black weeds, Florence became a weed herself in worth, a dandelion seed blown about by the winds of melancholy fortune.

All connected with mourning should be done in the simplest way possible.

”

separated ''' from you all, very trying """" circumstances, need to procure advice
almost in despair "" about everything except fussing over housekeeping
write in such a hurry as I have "" no comfort '''
''' forgive me ''' for so encroaching on your time, attention and kindness
’

I am your ''' poor ''' desolate and ''' afflicted child and friend ’ ”
‘ heart is solitary and '''lonely '''
no one can know how ''' severe our loss '''
or the ''' depth of misery ''' for us here

must go back to the beginning, a ''' melancholy business, '''
missing the ''' beloved and tender presence ''' of parent and ''' husband '''
house seems empty, forsaken, a deserted bird's nest
''' not one of my boys are companions '''

Send printed cards of thanks for sympathy shown. Notepaper should have thin black edge. ’

‘

plans for our sons ended with ''' his death '''
silent, I was decidedly adverse to that agenda ’
''' hear little from my boys '''
sometimes, give way to ''' weakness,'''' perplexities''' overcome me

“ <u>woman</u> is a very ''' helpless creature in this world ... '''
so completely unaccustomed to acting for myself for the last 34 years
''' ignorant of everything, become bewildered '''''
constantly forget things '''

always had with me those who could think & act for me
much better than I could for myself
''' miss the assistance of my children '''
''' ashamed ''' to send such useless uninteresting scrawl

Flowers need not be the formal white wreath, once the only correct thing.

’

William Stewart now the head of this family, soon to be married
home place at Auburn changed, never to be the same again
''' nothing will restore to me the loss I have had '''
intend to leave new couple to themselves, pay visits to daughters

family " ' much scattered and much reduced '''
house - my own for my life but ''' large and expensive ''' for single female
rejoice to give up management & profits to William
reserving own rooms for my use with liberty of coming/going as agreeable

''' from birth on, life is vicissitude and trial '''
loved friends give useful & judicious advice as to my arrangements
all helpful as are in unison with my own sentiments ...
expenses of Auburn ''' far beyond my power ''' ”

“

Flowers should be delivered to the house not earlier than the day before the funeral.

during separation, visits with Bessie, Anna and Ellen
decided to seek rented residence, adjoining family property, at Goodwood,
house new, pleasantly situated on 10 acres
for 3 year lease or from year to year as ''' life is uncertain ''' and sons will settle or ''' disperse '''

Willey ''' indolent ''' but must now become active, systematic master
matters have been ''' pressing on my mind
could think of nothing else night or day
difficult to know how to steer amidst so many interests & drawings of the ''' heart '''

''' confined almost entirely to house, ''' staid with Bessie
dear boys the subject of many prayers
''' disappointments, illnesses ''' while on path to pushing themselves on in life
love my dear girl children, uncomplaining, in trials and afflictions

Ordinary friends need attend at the church only; need not follow on to the cemetery.

necessity for exertion, always so much to be done & arranged
''' one's situation so changed, so alone ''' & obliged to think & act
without friend to think & act for or with us
as widows, we do feel our ''' desolation '''

he was ''' centre point of whole circle, to who all turned '''
& all looked to him for guidance and happiness
ready friend & councillor, life & spirit of every company
influenced, ruled and regulated whole country around us

Do not pay a call of condolence before the funeral.

ruled most ''' strictly ''' but so judiciously
never gave offense & ''' seldom appeared harsh '''
till the last year or two when affairs evidently affected his stretched
& overwrought mind, his feelings & actually his brain

allowed me ''' so long a portion of time '''
& ''' so large a portion of happiness ''' when
I am so ''' useless & unworthy … '''
redeem time now & try to do more good

mind more at ease - free from responsibility & exertion
of managing the establishment at Auburn
Auburn was advantageous to Willy, did more than had I remained
but is ''' lost to family now, from fraudulent dealings ''''''

One need not wear black but avoid a brightly-coloured frock.

Grandchildren, Willy & Harriette, wish I had sums to send you as Birthday gifts
''' fear it is out of my power, ''' now more than ever
new calls on my means
Anna requires ''' all I can spare ''' but truly love you, dears

''' stupid & tired, ''' cannot write decently my hand is so ''' weak '''
''' rheumatism ''' constantly for many weeks
''' cough & frailty ''' improved with milder weather
roads awfully bad, early dusk precludes visiting

make allowance for this epistle, almost unintelligible
''' asthma increases my deafness ''' so much I am a tax
on the kindness & patience of friends
''' poorly and out of breath, ''' grieved to be writing

Be as natural as possible. Do not assume a somber attitude.

young fry in house with cold weather
in one sitting room, continually run past my table
make such noise ‴ my poor ears ring with shrill loud voices ‴
‴ bad bilious headache makes me almost blind ′ ″

have not the ‴ means to pay the half
of what I am engaged to in debt ‴
rents are but a small help as are never fully paid
miss the boys very much – ‴ they hardly care now to come here ‴

‴ must deny myself much pleasure
reduced by adversity & loss of prosperity ‴ from different causes
money I have seems to melt ‴ like snow in sunshine ‴
& slides away in small divisions

Mourning clothes should be simply cut and made with materials with a dull surface.

"

have sent out little monies to Mama to buy some things for each of you
as Christmas presents, some little gift to every one
of my Grandchildren – ‴ a small sum to send so far ‴
but when each of the 42 have a little, makes a ‴ large total ‴

every year, ‴ less intercourse with friends
so few ever come to see us now ‴
every one of those with me in Ireland ‴ dead and gone ‴
except myself & two cousins who were wee children then

the first of June, ‴ 48 years ago, ‴ we sailed out
from Belfast for Canada
48 years is a good space out of the 76
I have been in this world

Crêpe, heavy veils, black-bordered handkerchiefs are no longer in vogue.

don't believe ‴ I shall ever see Peterboro' again
have not a present to send – could not travel to town
besides have not any money ‴
still my dear Frances, I give you blessings for many happy years ahead

‴ alone a great deal as deafness ‴ keeps me from joining in conversation
‴ mind is dull ‴ in consequence
enjoy reading, tho ‴ my sight is far from good ‴
no reason to complain for few women of 77 are as well

Official mourning periods are a matter of discretion.

"

DIED

STEWART – at Goodwood near Peterborough on the 24th ultimo, Frances Browne,
relict of the Hon. Thos. A. Stewart, in the 78th year of her age.
Peterborough Review, March 1, 1872:3.

New Chapters

from:
Roughing It in the Bush,
Susanna Moodie,
Chapter 27, "A Change in our Prospects"
and
Life in the Clearings versus the Bush,
Susanna Moodie, Chapter 1, "Belleville," 1854

Unfolding "New Chapters"

In this final poem, I wanted to represent the increased scope of possibilities experienced by the Moodie family once they left the Duoro woods. By creating a trumpet-like triangle, broadening at its base and almost bursting forth from the restrictions of the page, I wished to represent their new achievements in Belleville. My original piled text boxes within that triangle began to take on the connotation of festive gifts and in a moment of inspiration, I added a star to the top of my imagined Christmas tree. All these symbols, gifts, tree and star, spoke to me of the sense of new hope and inspiration that Susanna and family must have experienced. When my publisher formatted this poem, the text boxes were transformed into sprigged words spangling with optimism the spreading boughs of a pine or hemlock erected in the Moodie parlour. After surviving two fires in Douro, how ironic is it that Moodie has now the security and protection of a volunteer force in an emergency. And note the absurdity of her progression from paying debt from slim wardrobe reserves to a town which can outfit its fire fighters in red frock coats and white trousers. Susanna can even afford the health benefits of a long held dream, a steamer trip around the lake to Niagara when before, her husband had to borrow a side of mutton to save her life after the trials of delivery. Such rewards for such suffering …

h
ope
hope hope
hope hope hope
hope hope
hopehope
hope hope
ho pe

hope hope hope hope hope hope **hope hope hope hope hope**

hope **hope**

hope hope hope **hope hope hope**

hope hope **hope**

hope hope hope **hope hope hope**

hope hope hope **hope hope hope**

hope hope **hope hope**

hope **hope**

hope **hope hope**

First,
ten years
in the bush,
that great want, the want
of money, the insuperable and vast difficulties -
- Now, a score of years on, a peaceful
happy home, a haven of rest,
granted to us by Providence,
after the trials of Douro. Our small stone cottage with its screen
of hickory trees, in a town host to masts of sailing vessels,
substantial stone wharfs, valuable cargoes, wealthy merchants,
neat cottages with flower gardens, the brick or
limestone spires of four churches,
a large deep-toned sonorous bell (heard eight miles into the country,)
two fire engines worked by energetic teams of volunteers in tight-fitting frock-
coats of red, with white summer trousers and leather caps with long peaks
to protect them from injury, and lumberers on the river Moira,
where a mill owner lost 12,000 saw logs to the spring flood of 1852. Bridges
were threatened by a cow carried by the raging river.
Ill and languid, I am. A change of air was suggested for my recovering health and a trip
planned, my husband to accompany me on a streamer, "The Bay of Quinte," departing Belleville
and sailing first to Kingston, to fulfill my long-held hope, once an impossible dream, of
visiting the Falls of Niagara before I die. The steamer shall sail on to dock at Toronto which, in Indian,
literally means "Trees in the Water." How changed are our prospects since the militia
regiments were disbanded and Moodie, once more returned, to help me gather in our scant harvest.
A letter arrived from the Governor's secretary offering him the situation of sheriff. He looked upon it as a
gift sent from heaven to remove us from our sorrows and poverty.
From desperation to plenty, we have progressed …

hope hope hope hope hope hope hope **hopehope** **hope hope hope hope hope hope hope**
hopehope
hopehope
hopehope-

Afterword

As an undergraduate, more than fifty years ago, I was required to read Susanna Moodie's Roughing It in the Bush. I staggered through its five hundred pages wishing it were less long-winded but realizing that it represented seminal early Canadian writing - and by a female. One recorded incident particularly impressed me, the Chapter entitled *Fire*. I was moved by the determination and the resilience of one woman's struggle to protect home and family in a dreadful emergency. The words taken from Susanna's essays and the original letters of Catharine Parr Traill and Frances Stewart are re-used here in their exact form: grammar, spelling, short forms and underlining in the poems belong to those stalwart women of our past. The selection and configuration of their words, as well as the font size and spacing on the page, are my own interpretations.

I wish to extend thanks to poet Jordan Abel, for inspiring me, and to my professor and poet, Rob Taylor, who introduced me to the found-poem format, and for Rob's support and encouragement in undertaking this project. Thanks, too, to members of the Wednesday Writers, and to other friends in Mission, B.C., for critical commentary, and to publisher Kerry Coast for facilitating this publication.

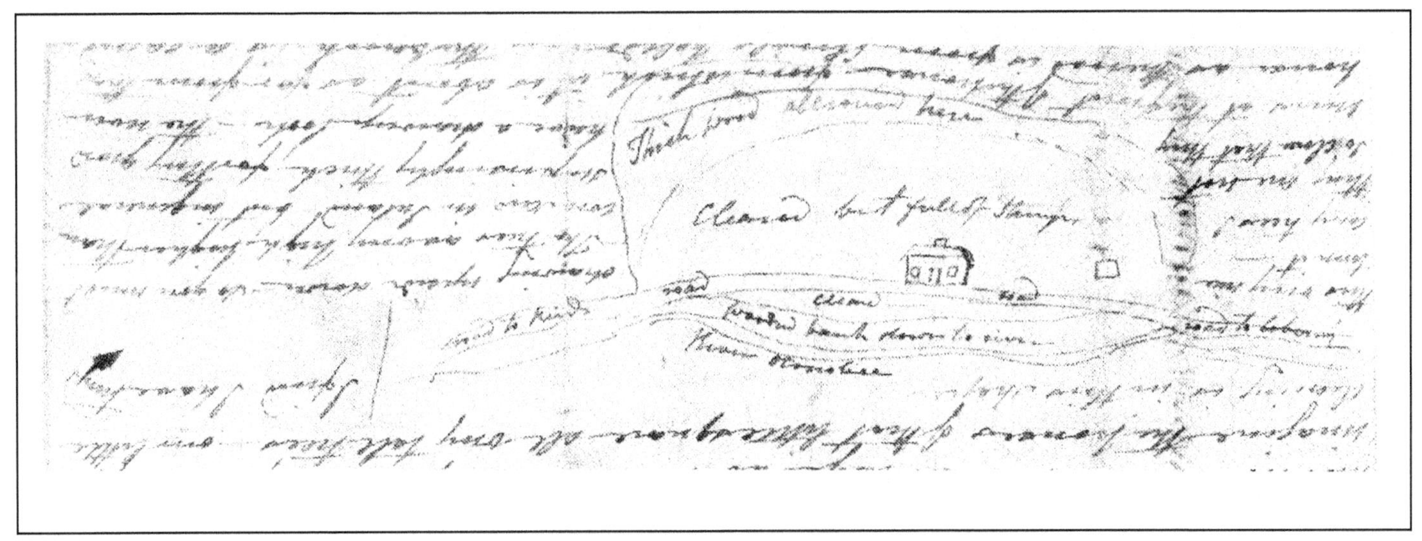

A sample of one of Frances Stewart's letters, as reprinted in Revisiting "Our Forest Home," The Immigrant Letters of Frances Stewart, Aoki, Jodi Lee, editor, Dundurn, Toronto, 2011.

Sources

Etiquette for Women, A Book of Modern Manners and Customs, Davison, Irene, Chancellor Press, London, 2002, first published, C. Arthur Pearson , Ltd. , 1928.

Life in the Clearings versus the Bush, Moodie, Susanna, McClelland and Stewart Inc.., Toronto, 1989, unabridged re-print of Life in the Clearings versus the Bush, London, 1854.

Revisiting "Our Forest Home," The Immigrant Letters of Frances Stewart, Aoki, Jodi Lee, editor, Dundurn, Toronto, 2011.

Roughing It in the Bush, Moodie, Susanna, McClelland and Stewart Inc., Toronto, 1989, unabridged re-print of Roughing It in the Bush, London, 1852.

The Backwoods of Canada, Parr Traill, Catharine, McClelland and Stewart Inc., Toronto, 1989, unabridged re-print of The Backwoods of Canada, London, 1836.